LEMURS!

Angie Marino

ILLUSTRATED BY
Kim (Greene) Murdock's 29 after school
art students

Dedication

This book is dedicated to all lemurs and
to those who use their time and energy to conserve them.
A.M. and K.G.M.

Angie and Kim are gladly donating the profit generated from the sale of this book to the Duke Lemur Center. Each child's lemur artwork may also be used for t-shirts, greeting cards and other related gift shop items for the sole benefit of the Duke Lemur Center. This fundraising opportunity is available to you, as well! Contact Kim Greene at kgreene@thebrighthorse.com for more information.

Acknowledgments

Our thanks go out to the 29 Brighthorse Afterschool Art students who contributed their unique illustrations, which ultimately inspired the making of this book. The variations in their drawings charmingly represent and celebrate the many differences among lemur species.

In addition, a dear appreciation to Lari Hatley, Niki Barnett, Greg Dye, David Haring, Andrea Katz, Steve Coombs, Julie McKinney and Lindsay Blancas from the Duke Lemur Center whom we spoke with personally. These individuals offered their time and expertise to make this book a reliable educational piece of literature.

There are no mistakes in art.

The original intent that seeded the idea for this book was the goal to celebrate children's artwork. We want children to see that there are no mistakes in art, that each piece is unique and equally valued. We invite all instructors to emphasize the illustrations in this book to encourage their students to be fearless as they work and to enjoy their outcome.

Word Watching

Rhyme:

We hear rhyme when the last parts of two words sound the same. Listen for pairs of words that rhyme in the large print. Find those pairs of words. Talk about how those two words look. Are their ending sounds spelled differently or the same? Find letter combinations that look different but sound the same.

Synonyms and Antonyms:

Synonyms are two words that mean the same or almost the same thing. Antonyms are two words that mean the opposite. Synonyms and antonyms help us know the meanings of new words in the text. Look for pairs of words in italics on various pages throughout the book. Decide if they are synonyms or antonyms.

Word Meanings

Dictionaries and glossaries tell us the meaning of words. You can also learn the meaning of words by using context clues or other words in the text that explain or state the meaning of the word. Notice the bold words throughout the book. Try to find the context clues that help you know the meaning. You can check your thoughts with the glossary at the back of the book to see if you were correct or not.

Madagascar is where they abound.
Some high in the trees. Some low to the ground.

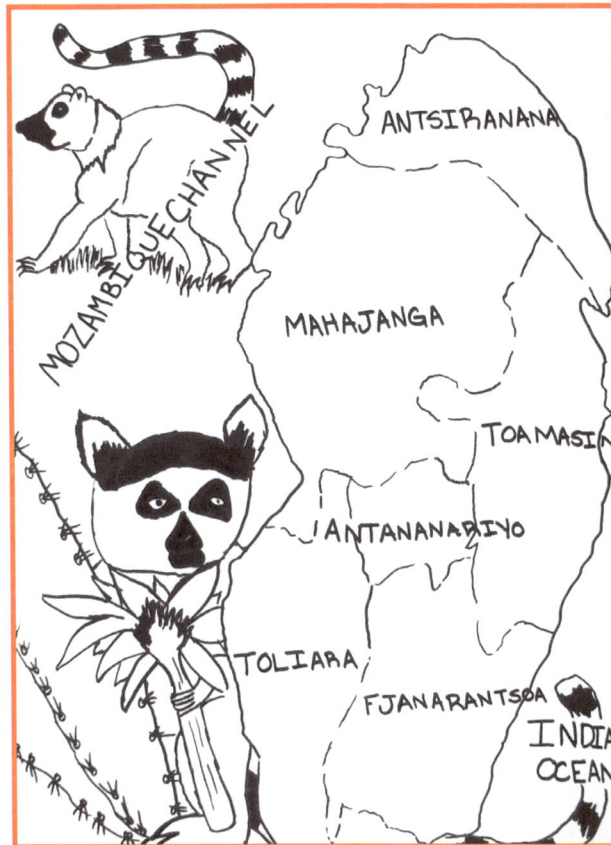

Zoe B., age 10

Lemurs live only in the wild in Madagascar. The largest population of lemurs outside of Madagascar is in North Carolina where the Duke Lemur Center hosts a number of lemurs. There they focus on research, conservation and education. All research at the center is **non-invasive**. That means that the researchers at the Duke Lemur Center don't ever harm the lemurs to learn more about them. Lemurs reside primarily up in trees and share the forests very well. Different **species** of lemurs prefer different levels of the forest. For example, the red-ruffed like the top layers of the forest canopy while the crowned lemurs are found in the lower level. Only a couple species of lemurs live mainly on the ground. The ring-tailed lemurs, for example, live on the ground because the trees in the "spiny" desert don't provide enough of what they need.

Is it a coon? Is it a cat?
What animal looks like that?

Luke V. age 10

Ring-tailed lemurs are often compared to raccoons because of their striped tails and the patches around their eyes. Ring-tailed lemurs as well as ruffed lemurs are said to *resemble* cats because of their size and fur. The male common black lemur also *looks like* a cat. It has yellow eyes, black fur and walks on all four legs with his tail and back raised up.

Like a skunk. Like a bat.
A rainbow tail. Look at that!

Jason Y. age 8

Lemurs are similar to skunks in that they are able to secrete a strong **scent** to mark territory and to communicate with others. They look nothing like bats, but several species of lemurs such as the aye-aye, are **nocturnal** like bats. That means they sleep during the day and are awake at night. In addition, nocturnal lemurs are similar to bats in that they use a process much like echolocation to find food. (You can find more on echolocation on page 17.) While lemurs don't actually have rainbow colored tails, their bodies and tails do vary in color according to species. Colors include black, brown, gray, white, cream, reddish brown and reddish orange. The ring-tailed lemurs are the only lemurs with stripes on their tails. The stripes are black and white.

Maybe a squirrel. Maybe a monkey.
A little thin. A little chunky.

Caroline K. age 7

The northern giant mouse lemur is said to be about the size of a squirrel. It walks on all four legs and hops from tree to tree like a squirrel. Some people may say lemurs act like monkeys because of their playful demeanor. They do have long tails like monkeys. However, lemurs are unable to hang or swing from their tails like some monkeys do. Instead, some lemurs use their tails for *storing* fat for long dry seasons when there is little food. During these long seasons their metabolic rate slows down. That means the rate at which they use their food is much slower. Their level of activity and their appetite for food also decrease. This behavior is called **torporing**. The fat tailed dwarf lemurs can gain and store up to 40% of its entire body weight of fat in their tails. Sometimes their tails get as big as the rest of their body. In Madagascar, there's a wet and dry season. During the dry season there's not a lot of food available. Resources are scarce so the fat-tailed lemurs tend to live off the fat stores in their tails.

Like to climb. Like to leap.
Hang on tight. Make a beep.

Brooke R. age 7

Lemurs have **grasping** hands and feet. They can grab and hold on tight to tree limbs and tree trunks. A few lemurs, such as the red-ruffed, black and white ruffed and sifaka (pronounced shi-fok) hang by their feet and reach for food with their hands. They can easily climb up, down, left or right using their tails for balance. The sifaka runs along tree branches and can nearly soar from tree to tree because of its unique ability to leap up to 20 feet. The coquerel's (pronounced kok-er-uh-l) sifaka has very long legs and short arms and is a **vertical** clinger and leaper. It jumps up and down rather then side to side.

Give a scent. Leave a trace.
Make a noise. Make a face.

Anna L. age 8

One way lemurs communicate is by leaving scent marks. They rub their scent glands against twigs or branches to mark group territory or feeding areas. As for noise, some species of lemurs make many different vocalizations to communicate including moan, chirp, purr, yip, cackle, squeal, bark, gulp and grunt. The crowned lemur has a piercing yap to help maintain contact with other lemurs of its kind. The ruffed lemur is the loudest of all the lemur species. Its alarm call can be heard over a half a mile away and alerts others of predators. It only takes one ruffed lemur to start the call. Then the others join in. Lemurs are also known for making facial expressions. The sifaka, for example, will start play by making an open-mouthed play face.

A curved tail waving in the air.
Slathered with a scent that none can bear.

Cecilia F. age 9

Lemurs' *scent* glands are found on various parts of their bodies depending on the species. The ring-tailed has scent glands on their wrists, near their armpits and at the base of their tail. Ring-tailed lemurs also have a sharp spur on each wrist gland to pierce tree branches before marking them. They do this in order to **embed** the scent securely into the tree so it's not easily washed off by rain and can last longer. The male red-bellied has a scent gland on top of its head which makes it look like he has greasy hair. Nearly all species have scent glands at the base of their tails. To compete for females, male ring-tailed and bamboo lemurs will cover their tails with a strong *odor* and "**waft**" them, or wave them back and forth, in their competitor's face.

Lemurs play. Lemurs tease.
Look at this one. It's a squeeze!

Theo P. age 6

Lemurs are known to be very *social* creatures. The **diurnal** lemurs, which are awake during the day, tend to live in small family groups of 3-10 members. These groups are called **troops**. The ring-tailed lemur is known to travel in larger troops of up to 30 lemurs. When traveling through their home, the ring-tailed will keep their tails raised to help keep all the members together. The aye-aye, which are nocturnal, are known to be more *solitary*. The northern giant mouse lemurs, also **nocturnal**, build spherical nests tightly between two tree forks. There they gather together to sleep.

Playful, bouncy, funky.
Jolly, fun and spunky.

Jade S. age 8

On the ground, the sifaka stands upright, holds its arms up high and hops to the side rather than head on. It's able to hop to the side on its legs because of its hip structure. This bouncing motion makes it look like it's dancing. For fun, the coquerel's sifaka, specifically, will occasionally descend to the ground to wrestle with other lemurs. Young lemurs will *initiate* play which helps them develop their social behaviors. *Starting* this play may bother some members of the lemur group but it almost always ends positively by each lemur grooming each other's fur.

Many colors, pink, blue and black.
A green and orange tail curved along its back.

Liam S. age 8

Just as the colors in this lemur drawing *vary*, the features of lemurs *differ* as well. There are any where from 70-100 or more different **species** of lemurs. They vary in size with the smallest species being the pygmy mouse lemur. An adult pygmy mouse lemur weighs about 35 grams (g) which is *approximately* the weight of a mouse. The largest species still living is the indri lemur. The indri weighs between 6 and 7.5 kilograms (kg) which is 13-17lbs, *about* the weight of an average sized cat. Lemurs are a part of the prosimian primates which means they originally existed before monkeys, apes and humans. They arrived to Madagascar around 60 million years ago. At that time none of the lemur species were in danger. Currently, 17 species are extinct and 75 species are endangered.

Lemurs red? Lemurs puffy?
Lemurs blue? Lemurs fluffy?

Amy R. age 5

When the aye-aye gets angry it can puff up its tail to make itself appear bigger. Red-tailed, black and white ruffed and red-bellied lemurs have thick fluffy fur. One might assume that their fur is meant to keep them warm. But actually, their fur helps keep them dry during the rainy seasons. Another type of lemur is the blue eyed black lemur. It is one of three primates that have the **recessive** gene for blue eyes. Humans and the brown spider monkey are the other two primates that can pass blue eyes down to their offspring.

A bright blue body. A night that's green.
The lemur name. What does it mean?

Colby P. age 7

The word lemur came from the Latin language and means ghosts. They were named this because of their reflective eyes, ghostly vocalizations and how quiet they are at night. Malagasy **folklore,** traditional Malagasy beliefs, legends or customs, are called "fady". A Malagasy fady says that an aye-aye pointing its long finger at someone is very bad luck. As a result, the aye-aye is the most feared by some Malagasy villagers.

A lemur's brain. An important part.
However small. It's very smart.

Hannah A. age 8

Lemurs are showing themselves to be intelligent. For example, studies at the Duke Lemur Center reveal that lemurs understand numbers and quantities without understanding language. In one study, lemurs were placed in front of a computer screen that showed two squares, each containing a different amount of red dots. Each time a lemur selected the square with the most red dots, a sweet pellet would drop. The lemurs were able to consistently choose the square with the most dots, earning them the sweet treat. In another test, a lemur was able to remember a sequence of pictures, even as long as two years after initially being shown the pictures.

Ring-tailed lemurs have black and white tails. Which ones are females? Which ones are males?

Avery T. age 10

Ring-tailed lemurs' tails always end in the color black. There is no **distinction** at all in the coloration between the male and female ring-tailed, ruffed, coquerel's sifaka, aye-aye, mouse or fat-tailed dwarf lemur. However, in some other lemur species, the males and females differ in color. The most obvious example is the blue-eyed black lemur. The males are black. The females are a reddish brown-gray. Interestingly, baby male lemurs are born the same color as their mother to camouflage the babies. This is the case for all male and female lemurs that differ in color. Another distinction between males and females is in the Sanford's lemur. The male has a cheek ruff while the female does not. The red-bellied male has white patches under its eyes while the female has no patches and a white belly. Finally, collared brown and mongoose lemurs have beards. The male mongoose lemur 's beard is reddish orange. The female's is white. The collared brown male and female both have an orange beard, but the male beard is thicker.

Aqua green. Aqua blue.
Tiny ears and purple too.

Arun K. age 8

Lemurs' ears vary in size. Most lemurs have *small* ears for their body size like the lemur illustrated on this page. The aye-aye, however, has very *large* ears. It uses them when looking for food. What the aye-aye does is tap branches and trunks of trees listening for *hollow* spots where insects and larvae can usually be found. The echo they hear indicates that the wood isn't solid but has an *empty* space where the insects and larvae can live. This process of hearing the echo is called **echolocation.** Page 29 will tell how aye-aye lemurs get the food out.

**Big wide eyes. A moist wet nose.
People like hands. People like toes.**

Melin W. age 6

Prosimians, which include lemurs, are the only primates to have *wet* noses. (Monkeys, humans and apes have dry noses). Like dogs and cats, who also have a *moist* nose, lemurs rely heavily on their sense of smell, particularly for communication. Each lemur's scent is different and gives off information. When another lemur detects the scent it can learn something about the other lemur. So lemurs get to know each other by giving off scents and smelling the same way people converse by talking and listening. Lemurs have hands and feet with pseudo (pronounced soo-doh) **opposable** thumbs. That means that their thumbs help them grasp or make a fist. Lemurs' fingers can't move independently of each other, so their hands work more like a mitten than a glove. Lemurs also have fingernails like humans except for their second finger which is a sharp claw used for grooming their fur.

Messy hair. It needs a comb.
Can't go out. Must stay home!

Michelle K. age 5

Lemurs have specialized bottom front teeth that grow outward (rather than upward) and are finely spaced just like a comb. Thus, these front incisors are known as a tooth comb. Lemurs use their tooth comb to groom most of their fur. Their grooming claw, sometimes call a toilet claw, on their hand is also used to scratch and *comb* fur, but just the hard to reach places where the tooth comb can't. Lemurs also use their toilet claw to clean their fur and pick out **external** parasites such as tics or fleas. If lemurs have a **spat** over food or space, they usually make up and end the verbal argument by using their tooth comb to *groom* each other.

Eyes far apart. Eyes nice and bright.
Eyes open wide. Eyes made for night.

Wyatt B. age 6

Lemurs' eyes are more **laterally** placed on their heads compared to their other primate cousins, such as monkeys, apes and humans. This means that they are off to the side more than in the center of their face. The nocturnal lemurs have especially keen vision to help them see and **forage** for food during the night. Their eyes are large and wide to help them absorb as much light as possible at night.

A look of worry. What does he see?
An enemy foe. What could it be?

Charles K. age 8

Fossas (pronounced foos-uh) are lemurs' main *predator* in Madagascar. Fossas are related to the mongoose family. They look like a mix of a weasel and a small mountain lion. Fossas can hunt in trees just as easily as on the ground. They can do this because they have the ability to climb up and back down, unlike most cats, making them especially skilled *hunters*. Sometimes fossas will work in groups to hunt larger lemurs. Some local Malagasy people say that fossas are dangerous and should be feared. Therefore, locals won't eat their meat, afraid that their bad characteristics will be passed onto the person who eats it.

A thick blue branch. Eyes looking back.
Could it be a fossa? Preparing to attack?

Kate B. age 7

Fossas are not the lemurs' only predator. They also have to be on guard for birds of prey, such as the harrier hawk or eagle and also for constricting snakes like a boa. During breeding season in southern Madagascar, male harrier hawks will hunt white Verreaux's sifakas and present them to the females to win their favor. Madagascar ground boas are larger and eat small mammals including lemurs. Madagascar tree boas are smaller and nocturnal. They eat nocturnal mammals like bats and small lemurs, such as the mouse and dwarf. Interestingly, there are no **venomous** snakes in Madagascar that would eat lemurs or inject venom into them.

A large red body. A tongue that's pink.
Eyes wide open. Do they blink?

David P. age 7

Lemurs don't typically stick out their tongues. But at the Duke Lemur Center there is a blue eyed black lemur named Olivier that walks around sticking his tongue out at others! Lemurs appear to be staring most of the time. They *actually* do blink contrary to what people may think. And like this particular lemur, they *truly* do have eye lashes, some longer than others.

A white fur coat. Thick with curl.
Pretty blue eyes. Looks like a girl!

Nora R. age 6

Most lemur species are **matriarchal,** meaning mother lemurs are in charge of the group. An older female lemur generally runs her **troop.** She also *chooses* the mate she will breed with. In addition, she gets the best food and most comfortable place to sleep. On chilly days lemurs love to take advantage of the morning sun to warm themselves up. When they do this, the female lemur in charge *selects* the nicest sunning spot.

Rump raised up. Belly hung down.
Maybe some babies. Heavy to the ground.

Lizzy P. age 10

Lemurs have one to six babies depending on the species. For most *diurnal* lemurs, babies will initially hang on the mother's stomach and then move to its mother's back for about 3 months. After this time the mothers will nip at the babies or refuse to give them a ride to encourage them to move on their own. Red-bellied males will help carry the offspring and may do so up to 100 days. For most *nocturnal* species the mother will *build* a nest for her young. The ruffed lemur is the only diurnal lemur that will make a nest. The mother will *construct* a nest at the top of the forest canopy. She will sit on her nest until its time to look for food. When she leaves the nest the father will sit on it. The babies will remain in the nest until she returns from **foraging**. Bamboo lemurs "park" their infants on a small branch in the middle of the bamboo grove.

Lemurs up high. Lemurs down low.
Lemurs in rain? Lemurs in snow?

Nick D. age 9

Madagascar has very unique and varied **ecosystems** which have ultimately produced over 70 species of lemurs. This is due to lemurs' ability to adapt to new *environments* and interact well with their *surroundings*. One way they help their ecosystem is by transporting seeds to new places. Ruffed lemurs eat a lot of fruit but don't digest the seeds and so the seeds are left in their feces. Lemurs also share the forests very well. Nearly every habitat in Madagascar consists of more than one lemur species. The lemurs are able to get along and remain there because they live at different levels of the forest and they eat different foods. Madagascar has two seasons, a dry season and a wet season. Lemurs will not typically encounter snow or extreme cold in their native land of Madagascar. When snow falls in Durham, North Carolina at the Duke Lemur Center, the lemurs remain warm inside where they can watch the snow through windows.

Looking for food? Looking for prey?
Dusk or dawn? What time of day?

June A. age 9

During the *dry* season food is *scarce*. During the *wet* season food is *plentiful*. Some lemurs will change their activity patterns or their diet to make it through the dry season. For example, mongoose lemurs will become nocturnal because specific flowers open at night. Other lemurs will become **crepuscular**, meaning active at dawn and dusk, to take advantage of food sources available at those times of day. Being active at dawn and dusk also helps ward off the summer heat.

One blue lemur. A little drowsy.
A long day of play. Now feeling lousy.

Sydney R. age 7

Lemurs typically nap after they eat. Some, like the ring-tailed lemur, sleep close together with others forming a ball of lemurs. Others, such as the ruffed lemur, sleep in trees spaced more widely apart. A pack of up to five fat-tailed dwarf lemurs will congregate in a tree hole. The female gray mouse lemurs gather together in nests or hallow areas in trees for daytime sleeping spots.

Red textured branch. A little like bamboo.
Do lemurs eat it? It may be hard to chew.

Maya V. age 7

There are 5 species of bamboo lemurs found in Madagascar that specialize in eating bamboo. Bamboo lemur teeth are sharp and **serrated.** They use their sharp saw-like teeth to cut through the hard outer layer of bamboo in order to eat the softer tastier center. Other lemurs eat mostly leaves and fruit and some sip **nectar**, the juice from a fruit or plant. Aye-aye enjoy larvae the most. It has rodent-like teeth that are constantly growing and enable it to *chew* through very hard surfaces such as brazil nuts or coconuts. It uses its teeth to *gnaw*, dig and chip away at wood to open a channel for getting food. Once it opens the tiny hole, the aye-aye uses its very thin middle finger to *scoop out* the larvae and insects. This middle finger has a **ball and socket joint,** just like the shoulder of a human, so it is able to move in almost any direction to *dig out* the food.

Here's a lemur on bamboo.
He's gripping tight and eyeing you.

Walker B. age 7

While lemurs are very social animals they do not make good pets. They don't litter train. In addition, they have very sharp teeth and can become aggressive towards people. If you are walking around in a rural village or park in Madagascar you may see a lemur leaping around in the trees fairly near you. The gray mouse lemur has been seen at night in gardens and in brush along the side of the roads in Madagascar. Lemurs in the wild, though, don't typically approach people.

Lemurs die out from deforestation.
Green green green for reforestation!

Nicholas M. age 7

Lemurs are the most endangered primate in the world. Due to human population growth, poverty and international demand, many forests in Madagascar are being cut down for farmland and for their precious woods. Also, there is a rise of interest to eat lemurs. Their meat is called "bush meat.". Thankfully, there are ways we can help prevent lemurs from further damage or extinction. The Duke Lemur Center (DLC) is working with Malagasy farmers to come up with more sustainable methods of agriculture. One method is call agriforestry where farmers actually farm fruit trees. Another method is learning how to grow more rice on less land. The System of Rice Intensification (SRI) is being taught throughout Madagascar. Third is ecotourism. Ecotourism is inviting tourists to visit the forests and lemurs that are there. This can generate income for local communities and preserve the forests. Last is education. The Madagascar Fauna Group (MFG) trains teachers about the danger lemurs are in and how to preserve them. The teachers then inform children and families in their communities.

Lemurs alive! Lemurs free!
You can help keep them be!

Zoe B. age 9

One way to support lemurs is telling other people what you've learned about them. This brings awareness about lemurs' critical situation. To see lemurs up close, the Duke Lemur Center welcomes you to attend an educational tour. There are tours for all ages and tailored to specific interests. You can learn more about the tours by contacting the Duke Lemur Center using their website listed on the next page. Another way to support lemurs is by donating directly to different conservation organizations that are working to protect habitats for all Madagascar's plants and animals. Three conservation organizations are:

The Duke Lemur Center:
http://lemur.duke.edu

Madagascar Fauna Group:
www.savethelemur.org

Simpona:
www.simpona.org

Glossary

ball and socket joint (p.29) ....where the end of a bone fits into another bone shaped like a cup. The cup enables the connecting bone to move in almost any direction, up, down, left, right and in a circular motion. On humans, the shoulder and hip are ball and socket joints.

crepuscular (p.27) ....active at dawn, when the sun is coming up, or at dusk, when the sun is going down

distinction (p.16) ....difference between two things

diurnal (p.10).........................animals that are awake during the day and asleep at night

echolocation (p.17)................finding a person, place or object by hearing an echo

ecosystems (p.26).................a system where living organisms interact with their environment

embed (p.9) ....to press securely into another object

external (p.19) ....on the outside of something

forage (p.20, 25) ....to look for food

folklore (p.14) ....stories passed down from one generation to another

grasping (p.7)........................grabbing a hold of something with hands or feet

Glossary (cont.)

laterally (p.20) .... on the side of a person or object

matriarchal (p.24) .... when a group of animals follows a female rather than a male

nectar (p.29) .... the sweet juice found in plants or fruit

nocturnal (p.5, 10) .... animals that are asleep during the day and awake at night

non-invasive (p.3) .... not entering or harming the lemurs' bodies

opposable (p.18) .... being placed opposite, or facing something else

scent (p.5) .... an odor or smell

serrated (p. 29) .... jagged, like the teeth of a saw

spat (p.19) .... a small argument

species (p.3, 12) .... kinds or types

torpor (p.6) .... be inactive for a long period of time to let the body rest

troop (p.10, 24) .... a family or group of lemurs

venomous (p.22) .... containing poison that can be injected

vertical (p.7) .... in an up-down direction

waft (p.9) .... to wave lightly back and forth

Author/Illustrator Page

Angie Marino, a native of Elkhart, Indiana, received her BS in Elementary Education at DePaul University in Chicago, IL. She has loved rhyme for as long as she can remember. The first book she remembers enjoying was *Cat in the Hat* by Dr. Seuss. At a very young age she began writing her own rhymes and has a collection of poems she has written for friends and family members. She also loves learning, which is why she had so much fun writing *LEMURS!*. She didn't know much about lemurs when she first began this book. Angie currently resides in Chapel Hill, NC where she teaches and enjoys her family.

Kim (Greene) Murdock has owned and operated Bright Horse Art, Inc., a community focused small business that offers art programming to children ages 5-15 at several locations in Chapel Hill, since 2007. Through her afterschool art program Kim met third grade teacher Angie Marino. Each was inspired by the other's specialized skills and in 2011 joined forces to create this book. Kim also combines her lifelong passion for horses and art in her work as Art Director at Bright Horse Farm and Art Studio in Pittsboro, NC, a company she co-founded in 2007 with business partner Cindy McWilliams.

www.ingramcontent.com/pod-product-compliance
Lightning Source LLC
Chambersburg PA
CBHW041546040426
42447CB00002B/66